WORLD'S FASTEST ANIMALS

T0014780

APEX

BY BRIENNA ROSSITER

WWW.APEXEDITIONS.COM

Copyright © 2022 by Apex Editions, Mendota Heights, MN 55120. All rights reserved. No part of this book may be reproduced or utilized in any form or by any means without written permission from the publisher.

Apex is distributed by North Star Editions:
sales@northstareditions.com | 888-417-0195

Produced for Apex by Red Line Editorial.

Photographs ©: Shutterstock Images, cover, 1, 4–5, 6–7, 8, 9, 10–11, 12, 13, 14–15, 15, 16–17, 18, 19, 22–23, 24–25, 26, 27, 29; Ann Froschauer/USFWS, 20–21

Library of Congress Control Number: 2021918556

ISBN
978-1-63738-169-4 (hardcover)
978-1-63738-205-9 (paperback)
978-1-63738-273-8 (ebook pdf)
978-1-63738-241-7 (hosted ebook)

Printed in the United States of America
Mankato, MN
012022

NOTE TO PARENTS AND EDUCATORS

Apex books are designed to build literacy skills in striving readers. Exciting, high-interest content attracts and holds readers' attention. The text is carefully leveled to allow students to achieve success quickly. Additional features, such as bolded glossary words for difficult terms, help build comprehension.

TABLE OF CONTENTS

CHAPTER 1

BUILT FOR SPEED

A cheetah sees a springbok. The cheetah starts to run. It goes from 0 to 60 miles per hour (0–97 km/h) in just three seconds.

A cheetah can go 7 miles per hour (11 km/h) faster with every stride.

The cheetah's tail stretches out behind it. This helps the cat balance. And its sharp claws grip the ground.

Big cats run fast for short bursts. Lions can reach 50 miles per hour (80 km/h).

A cheetah's long leg muscles help it run fast.

But soon, the cheetah gets tired. It must slow down. The springbok escapes. After a rest, the cheetah will hunt again.

Cheetahs and springboks are both medium-sized animals. Their size allows them to go fast.

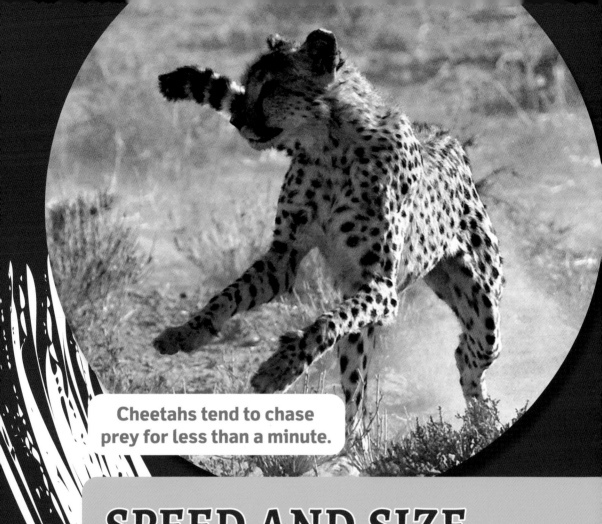

Cheetahs tend to chase prey for less than a minute.

SPEED AND SIZE

Small animals speed up quickly. But their top speed is low. Big animals have long legs and strong muscles. But they use up their energy quickly. So, medium-sized animals tend to be fastest.

CHAPTER 2

FASTEST ON LAND

The cheetah is the fastest land animal. Its top speed is more than 71 miles per hour (114 km/h). It also **accelerates** the fastest.

Cheetahs are able to make quick turns without losing speed.

Cheetahs hunt some of the other swiftest animals. Wildebeests can run 50 miles per hour (80 km/h). Springboks can go 55 miles per hour (89 km/h).

Wildebeests are also known as gnus.

Pronghorns live in the grasslands of North America.

LONG DISTANCE

Pronghorns are the fastest long-distance runners. They can run more than 55 miles per hour (89 km/h) for miles. Pads on their hooves help them run on hard ground.

Greyhounds are the second-fastest accelerators. They can reach their top speed after just three steps.

Greyhounds can run 45 miles per hour (72 km/h).

Fast animals have several traits in common. They have long legs. And they have **sleek** bodies.

Ostriches can sprint 43 miles per hour (69 km/h).

An ostrich's long legs can cover 16 feet (5 m) in one step.

CHAPTER 3

FASTEST IN THE AIR

The peregrine falcon is the fastest animal in the sky. This bird **dives** while hunting. It can go up to 200 miles per hour (322 km/h).

The peregrine falcon folds its wings and plunges down toward its prey.

When flapping their wings, peregrine falcons only go about 60 miles per hour (97 km/h).

When flying **level**, other birds beat falcons. Common swifts go 69 miles per hour (111 km/h). Albatrosses might be even faster.

The horsefly is the fastest insect. It can fly 90 miles per hour (145 km/h).

Scientists think one type of swift might fly as fast as 105 miles per hour (169 km/h). But this speed has never been measured.

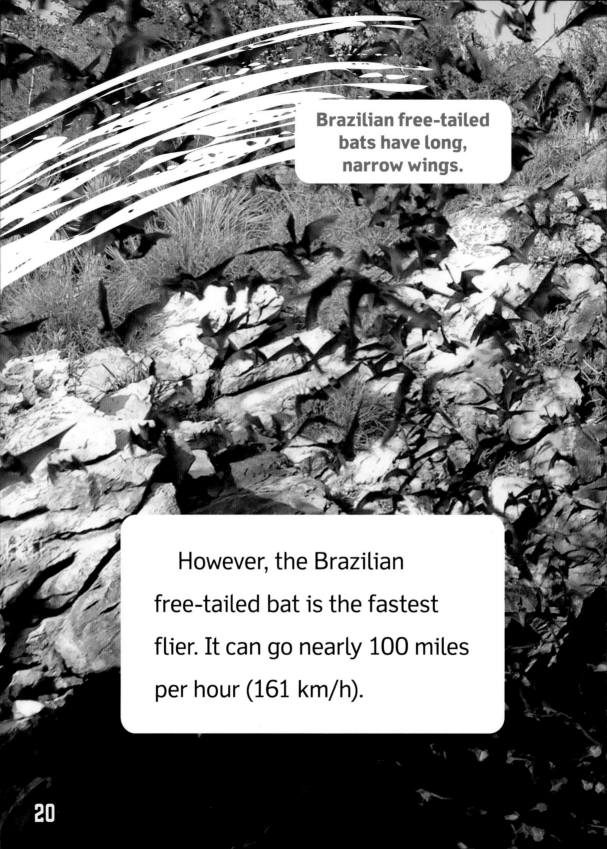

Brazilian free-tailed bats have long, narrow wings.

However, the Brazilian free-tailed bat is the fastest flier. It can go nearly 100 miles per hour (161 km/h).

TRACKING THE FASTEST BATS

Scientists put trackers on bats. Then they flew an airplane near a bat cave. The plane picked up the trackers' signals. This showed the bats' movements.

CHAPTER 4

FASTEST IN THE WATER

Scientists disagree about the fastest swimmer. Some choose the sailfish. It can reach 68 miles per hour (109 km/h) when leaping.

Sailfish are known for their large fins that look similar to sails.

Marlin are some of the biggest fish on Earth. Like sailfish, they have long, pointed snouts.

Others choose the marlin. This fish might swim 80 miles per hour (129 km/h). Both these fish have long, **streamlined** bodies.

FOLDING FINS

A sailfish has several long fins. It folds two side fins back while it swims. They fit in **grooves** on its body. This lessens **drag**.

The fastest sea **mammals** are orcas. They can swim more than 55 miles per hour (89 km/h). They can also dive deep underwater.

The orca's speed makes it a fierce hunter.

A mako shark's pointed snout helps it cut quickly through water.

The fastest shark is a mako shark. It can go about 45 miles per hour (72 km/h).

COMPREHENSION QUESTIONS

Write your answers on a separate piece of paper.

1. Write a sentence describing how an animal's size relates to its top speed.

2. Would you want to race a cheetah? Why or why not?

3. Which animal is the fastest long-distance runner?

   A. cheetah
   B. greyhound
   C. pronghorn

4. Why would having long legs help an animal run quickly?

   A. The animal would have smaller leg muscles.
   B. The animal would cover more ground with each step.
   C. The animal would be more likely to fall.

5. What does **traits** mean in this book?

*Fast animals have several **traits** in common. They have long legs. And they have sleek bodies.*

    A. details about how something looks
    B. facts about where something lives
    C. plans for the future

6. What does **swiftest** mean in this book?

*Cheetahs hunt some of the other **swiftest** animals. Wildebeests can run 50 miles per hour (80 km/h).*

    A. slowest
    B. fastest
    C. sleepiest

Answer key on page 32.

GLOSSARY

accelerates
Speeds up.

dives
Folds its wings and moves down very quickly through the air.

drag
The force of air or water pushing back against a moving object.

grooves
Dips or cuts that are shaped like long, thin lines.

level
At the same height.

mammals
Animals that have hair and produce milk for their young.

sleek
Having a shape that cuts through the air.

streamlined
Shaped to move quickly and easily through air or water with very little drag.

TO LEARN MORE

BOOKS

Chanez, Katie. *Marlin*. Mendota Heights, MN: Apex Editions, 2021.

Geister-Jones, Sophie. *Cheetahs*. Mendota Heights, MN: Apex Editions, 2021.

Olson, Elsie. *Animal Speed Showdown*. Minneapolis: Abdo Publishing, 2020.

ONLINE RESOURCES

Visit **www.apexeditions.com** to find links and resources related to this title.

ABOUT THE AUTHOR

Brienna Rossiter is a writer and editor who lives in Minnesota. She enjoys reading about animals and science.

INDEX

Answer Key:
1. Answers will vary; **2.** Answers will vary; **3.** C; **4.** B; **5.** A; **6.** B